Hiking

BY M. J. YORK

Published by The Child's World®
1980 Lookout Drive • Mankato, MN 56003-1705
800-599-READ • www.childsworld.com

Acknowledgments
The Child's World®: Mary Berendes, Publishing Director
Red Line Editorial: Editorial direction
The Design Lab: Design
Amnet: Production

Photographs ©: Shutterstock Images, cover (top right), cover
(bottom right), back cover (left), 1 (top right), 1 (bottom right),
3, 9, 12, 16, 17; Hurst Photo/Shutterstock Images, cover
(center), 1 (center); PhotoDisc, back cover (right), 11; Purestock/
Thinkstock, back cover (bottom), 7; Creatas/Thinkstock, 4–5;
Rafa Irusta/Shutterstock Images, 6; William Silver/Shutterstock
Images, 8; DigitalVision, 10; Jeff Metzger/Shutterstock Images,
13; Eric Isselee/Thinkstock, 14; Thinkstock, 18; RJ Lerich/
Shutterstock Images, 19; Stefano Lunardi/Thinkstock, 20–21

ISBN 9781626873308
LCCN 2014930667

Printed in the United States of America
Mankato, MN
July, 2014
PA02222

ABOUT THE AUTHOR

M. J. York is a children's author and editor who lives in Minnesota. She has loved the outdoors her entire life and started camping, hiking, and canoeing at a young age.

CONTENTS

TAKING A HIKE

Have you ever taken a long walk in the
woods? Maybe you followed a trail along
a beach or around a lake. Or maybe you
scrambled around rocks while climbing a
mountain path.

There's a lot to see on a hike through the woods.

Many people love to hike. They enjoy spending time in nature. They breathe the fresh air. Sometimes, they see wild animals or interesting trees and flowers. Hiking lets people see **scenic** views and natural wonders. They take photos or get ideas for art projects. Hiking is great exercise, too!

WHAT IS HIKING?

Hiking is walking for fun or fitness. Hiking is usually done in nature, not in the city. People usually hike on trails. Walking on city streets or sidewalks is not usually called hiking.

People can hike if they are young or old. **Athletic** or not, anyone can hike. There are even trails people in wheelchairs can use.

Sometimes, people hike alone. Or, people hike with friends or family.

Hiking is a part of many outdoor activities. People go on hikes when they go camping. Rock climbers hike to their climbing sites. Hunters hike to their hunting grounds.

HIKING CLUBS

People can join hiking clubs to find new hiking companions. Hiking club leaders plan hikes for the group. Some hiking clubs, such as the Appalachian Mountain Club, are more than 100 years old.

People of all ages enjoy hiking.

HIKING TRAILS

Hikes can be very short. Some only last an hour or an afternoon. They can be much longer, too. Hikes can last a whole day or even many days. A hike lasting one day or less is called a day hike.

The Appalachian Trail passes through Great Smoky Mountains National Park in the southeastern United States.

Short trails might be one mile (1.6 km) or less. A mile-long hike takes about half an hour. A hike takes longer if it is uphill. Hiking uphill can be difficult and slow hikers down. Rough **terrain** makes people hike more slowly, too.

Some trails are so long they cross several states. The Appalachian Trail and the Pacific Crest Trail are two famous ones. The Appalachian Trail is in the eastern United States. It runs through the Appalachian Mountains. The Pacific Crest Trail is on the West Coast. They are each more than 2,000 miles (3,200 km) long!

BACKPACKING
People who hike for more than one day must camp on the trail. This is called backpacking. Backpackers carry everything they need in a backpack. This includes a tent, spare clothing, food, and cooking gear.

Take a small backpack with you on a day hike.

WHERE DO PEOPLE HIKE?

The starting point of a hiking trail is called the trailhead. Some trails make a loop. If you follow the entire trail, you end up back at the trailhead. Some trails go from the trailhead to a different end point. On these trails, people walk back over

You can hike across deserts, near water, and in the mountains.

the same ground to return to the trailhead. Or, they need **transportation** home.

Many trails go to scenic locations. They might lead up to a mountain overlook or go to a waterfall. People hike through every **environment**. They go over every type of terrain. Hikers **trek** along beaches, across deserts, and through forests. They climb mountains and cross prairies.

HIKING YEAR ROUND

There are good reasons to hike in every season.
- In spring, leaves turn green. Baby animals are born. There are fewer bugs.
- In summer, active animals are easier to spot. The days are long. Wildflowers are blooming.
- In fall, leaves turn different colors. The days are cooler, so hiking is comfortable.
- In winter, there are no bugs. Trails have fewer people. Animal tracks are easy to find in the snow.

Enjoy fall colors on an autumn hike.

HIKING GEAR

It does not take much special gear to hike. People need sturdy shoes or boots. Sneakers are fine for short hikes. People hiking long distances often wear hiking boots. Hiking boots support their feet and ankles.

Hikers also need clothing to protect them from the weather. They wear several layers to keep warm and dry. It is not a good idea to wear blue jeans or cotton clothes. These make you colder if you get wet. A hat and sunscreen keep off the sun. Bug spray keeps mosquitoes and ticks away.

People hiking in the mountains or on uneven ground often bring hiking poles.

Sturdy hiking boots help hikers avoid foot and ankle problems.

Hiking poles help hikers keep their balance. Poles make hiking easier because they make your arms help out your legs.

Hikers bring all their gear in a backpack. It is important to bring plenty of water. Snacks, a map and **compass**, and a first aid kit are all smart things to bring, too.

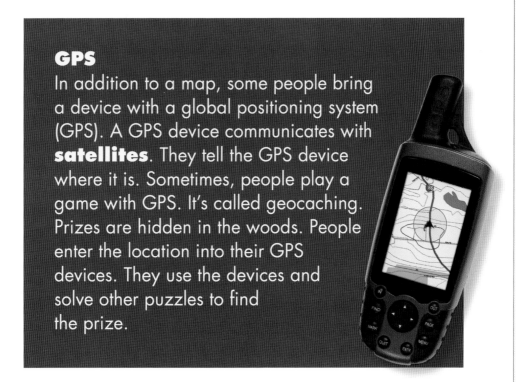

GPS

In addition to a map, some people bring a device with a global positioning system (GPS). A GPS device communicates with **satellites**. They tell the GPS device where it is. Sometimes, people play a game with GPS. It's called geocaching. Prizes are hidden in the woods. People enter the location into their GPS devices. They use the devices and solve other puzzles to find the prize.

GPS devices help hikers find their way.

STAYING SAFE OUTDOORS

People can have accidents while they are hiking. But planning and being careful can prevent most problems.

Most animals are not a threat. But bears, cougars, and other animals are sometimes dangerous. People can avoid animals by making noise. Animals hear the noise before they see

Encountering a cougar on a hike is very rare.

the people. They run away and leave the people alone. People in groups are usually safe, too.

Most snakes are not dangerous. Only a few types of **venomous** snakes live in North America. When hikers see a snake, they should back up. Then they should wait for it to move. Or they may go far around it. Never poke a snake with a stick.

POISON IVY AND POISON OAK

Watch out for plants with leaves growing in groups of three. These plants could be poison ivy or poison oak. They grow where the soil has been dug up. Look for them along the edges of forests and trails. Touching these plants can cause an itchy rash.

A survival kit helps when people get lost or stay out later than planned. A survival kit should have a flashlight or headlamp. It should have a pocketknife and a lighter or matches. It needs a whistle and a mirror to signal for help. A survival kit should have something for extra shelter. This might be a tent, a sleeping bag, or a **space blanket.**

A space blanket can help keep you warm in an emergency.

Matches, water, and extra batteries are just a few things that should be in your survival kit.

AVOIDING INJURIES

Hiking is an active sport that can cause **injuries**. Hikers try to prevent these accidents. They wear comfortable shoes or boots. They keep their laces tied tightly. Hikers slow down if the terrain is rough. They drink plenty of water. They rest when they get tired.

Be careful hiking on rocky trails.

Sometimes, hikers scramble over rocks or down steep slopes. Falling can cause injuries. Hikers keep one or both hands on a rock or tree to prevent falls. They test where they put their hands or feet. This helps them make sure the rock or tree can take their weight.

Blisters form when boots or socks rub against the skin. Hikers should break in new shoes or boots before a long hike. This means wearing them for longer and longer amounts of time until they are comfortable. Wearing sock liners under hiking socks helps, too. Hikers can use moleskin, a type of cloth with a sticky back. It will protect blisters that do form.

TAKING CARE OF NATURE

Hikers can protect nature and enjoy it at the same time. Do not pick plants or take anything home with you. Do not leave anything behind. Remember: Take only photos and leave only footprints!

Wear thick hiking socks with your boots to prevent blisters.

OUT IN NATURE

Hiking is a great way to get outside and enjoy nature. People see beautiful sights. They may see a field of wildflowers or a babbling brook. If they're lucky, they might spot a mother deer with her fawn. Hikers might go deep into

Hiking helps you see nature's beauty.

the **wilderness**. Or, they might discover something new in a nearby park.

Hiking teaches people about nature. Hikers can see the seasons changing. They watch how birds and animals behave. After hiking, they care more about nature and the environment. Hiking can help people be happier and healthier for their whole lives.

GLOSSARY

athletic (ath-LET-ik): An athletic person is trained in or is good at sports or physical fitness. A person does not have to be athletic to enjoy the outdoors.

compass (KUM-puhs): A compass is a device that shows which way is north. People use a map and a compass to find their way.

environment (en-VYE-run-munt): The environment is the natural world that surrounds living things. Protect the environment by not littering.

injuries (IN-jur-ees): Injuries are harm or damage done to a body. Avoid injuries by using the right gear.

satellites (SAT-uh-lites): Satellites are spacecraft circling Earth. Cell phones and other devices use satellites to communicate.

scenic (SEE-nik): Something scenic is beautiful to look at. Hikers may get scenic views of a mountain.

space blanket (SPAYS BLANG-kit): A space blanket is an emergency wrap made of a shiny material that holds in heat. A space blanket can keep someone warm if they get lost.

terrain (tuh-RAYN): Terrain is the features of an area of land. Hike carefully over rocky terrain.

transportation (trans-pur-TAY-shun): Transportation is a way of moving people or things from one place to another. Cars and bikes are all means of transportation.

trek (trek): To trek is to take a difficult walk or hike. The backpackers will trek through the wilderness.

venomous (VEN-uh-mus): Something that is venomous has a bite that can poison people or animals. Do not get close to venomous snakes.

wilderness (WIL-dur-nis): Wilderness is wild land where few people live or visit. Some people go backpacking in the wilderness.

TO LEARN MORE

BOOKS

Loy, Jessica. *Follow the Trail: A Young Person's Guide to the Great Outdoors.* New York: Henry Holt, 2003.

McKinney, John. *Let's Go Geocaching.* New York: DK Publishing, 2008.

National Geographic Kids National Parks Guide USA: The Most Amazing Sights, Scenes, and Cool Activities from Coast to Coast. Washington, DC: National Geographic, 2012.

WEB SITES

Visit our Web site for links about hiking:
childsworld.com/links

Note to Parents, Teachers, and Librarians: We routinely verify our Web links to make sure they are safe and active sites. So encourage your readers to check them out!

INDEX